Light Is the Odalisque

Light Is the Odalisque

Poems

LaWanda Walters

Press 53
Winston-Salem

Press 53, LLC
PO Box 30314
Winston-Salem, NC 27130

First Edition

Copyright © 2016 by LaWanda Walters

Silver Concho Poetry Series
edited by Pamela Uschuk and William Pitt Root

All rights reserved, including the right of reproduction in
whole or in part in any form except in the case of brief quotations
embodied in critical articles or reviews. For permission, contact
publisher at editor@Press53.com, or at the address above.

Cover design by Kevin Morgan Watson

Cover art, "Odalisque," Copyright © 2009
by Mark Andres, used by permission of the artist.

Author photo by Tess Despres Weinberg

Printed on acid-free paper
ISBN 978-1-941209-39-4

To my children, Tess and Jason,
and in memory of their father, David R. Weinberg

and to John Philip Drury

Acknowledgments

Some of the poems in this book first appeared in the following magazines, to whose editors I am deeply grateful:

The Antioch Review: "The Danger of These Lines You Wrote," "Her Art," and "My Life at the Convenience Store"
The Cincinnati Review: "Ode to Joy's Friend"
Cultural Weekly: "'Rosebud,' He Whispered," and "Falling All Those Stories Down"
Cutthroat: "The Exact Coordinates of Hell," "Handling Her Clothes," and "Ode to de Kooning's Penis"
Danse Macabre: "How Girls Walk through the Eye of a Needle," "Ship in a Bottle," and "Widow's Walk"
The Georgia Review: "Demeter's Escape," "Fig," "Goodness in Mississippi," and "Mysterious Barricades" (under the title "The Barricade")
Iodine Poetry Journal: "On Seeing a Photograph of Klimt's *Schubert at the Piano*, Destroyed by Fire," "Trying to Write a Love Poem for You, I Write about the Father of My Children," and "Unmade Bed"
The Laurel Review: "The True Story"
North American Review: "Orpheus and Eurydice at the AWP" (under the title "Orpheus and Eurydice Have a Bad Vacation") and "That Poem about Your Ex's Breasts"
Ploughshares: "Marilyn Monroe"
Shenandoah: "Piano Legs"
Southern Poetry Review: "On Being Alive at the Same Time" and "The Good China" (under the title "Grandmother's Blue Willow Dishes")
Sou'wester: "Bloodletting"

"Goodness in Mississippi" also appeared in *The Best American Poetry 2015* (Scribner, 2015), edited by Sherman Alexie and David Lehman.

"Marilyn Monroe" was reprinted in *Obsession: Sestinas in the Twenty-First Century* (Dartmouth College Press, 2014), edited by Carolyn Beard Whitlow and Marilyn Krysl.

"Her Art" was chosen for *Best New Poets* (Meridian, 2007), edited by Natasha Trethewey.

Table of Contents

I

Goodness in Mississippi	3
Marilyn Monroe	4
Fig	6
Rescuing My Sister	8
The Good China	9
Hattiesburg	11
How Girls Walk through the Eye of a Needle	12
Bloodletting	13
Paperback Rider	16
June 1969	19
First Love	20
First Marriage	22
Ship in a Bottle	24
The Exact Coordinates of Hell	25
The True Story	26

II

Mysterious Barricades	31
My Life at the Convenience Store	32
Party Float	35
Orpheus and Eurydice at the AWP	37
That Poem about Your Ex's Breasts	38
Two-Part Invention	39
Trying to Write a Love Poem for You, I Write About the Father of My Children	40
On Being Alive at the Same Time	41
Falling All Those Stories Down	43
Widow's Walk	44
Demeter's Escape	46
Lost Painting	48

III

Unmade Bed	53
Brake, Brake, Brake, Ephemeral Car	55
Short Story Based on a David Hockney Painting	58
Ode to de Kooning's Penis	60
The Girl Taking Jackson Pollock's Picture	62
Sidewalk Art on Wall Street	66
Tortoise and Hare in the Museum	67
The Painter at Noon	69
Available Beauty	71

IV

Her Art	77
Piano Legs	79
On Seeing a Photograph of Klimt's *Schubert at the Piano*, Destroyed by Fire	82
Ode to Joy's Friend	84
House Cats	86
"Rosebud," He Whispered	88
Stanislavsky's Method	89
Handling Her Clothes	90
How a Poem Can Staunch a Wound	93
A Piece of Work	94
The Woman Who Was Almost My Sister-in-Law	98
The Danger of These Lines You Wrote	101
A Note from the Author	105
Author biography	107
Cover artist biography	109

How far must our mother run to escape from her grief?

That's aesthetic distance.

> William Matthews
> *Foreseeable Futures*

I

Goodness in Mississippi

> After Gwendolyn Brooks's "We Real Cool,"
> with thanks to Terrance Hayes

My friend said I wasn't fat but she was, and we
would go on that way, back and forth. She was my first real

friend, the kind who changes everything. Her mother was so cool,
didn't shave down there for the country club pool where we

sat beside her. I saw a gleam of her secret, silver hair and was left
dreaming of lime floating in a clear drink. I started saying hi at school

and people smiled back. Smile first, my friend said, and we
were a team. The cheerleaders who would always lurk

by the field, showing off their muscled legs—of late
I'd hardly noticed them. We talked about art, we

attended science camp in Gulfport. That's where her mother got struck
by a car the next year. She must have thrown the new baby straight

as a football to save her. Their family was on vacation, and we
found out at Sunday School, waiting for the choir to sing.

She was so good she comforted *me*. People saying, "It's just a sin,"
her mom like Snow White under glass, red lipstick, platinum hair we

knew was genetic. You'll still look young, I said. I think you're thin.
We'd skip lunch, drink Sego ("good for your ego"). Last year I drank gin

and called her ex. "She passed," he drawled, like it was the weather. We
tried powdered donuts with the Sego, sweated to the Beatles and jazz.

Her whole life was beginning. We moved away from there one June,
Mississippi tight-mouthed as a lid on fig preserves. And we—

we white girls—knew nothing. The fire-bombed store, the owner who died
for paying his friends' poll taxes. Anorexia would be famous soon.

Marilyn Monroe

I didn't know much about Marilyn
Monroe the day she died. I'd heard
her name. The world's most beautiful woman
has killed herself, said the newscaster.
I saw her stretcher on the black-and-white
television. I was visiting

my cousin's fiancé's house—visiting
strangers. But the news about Marilyn
had me squeezed on the couch in that white
farmhouse of Jan's fiancé's herd
of brothers. And while the newscaster
talked, Jan's fiancé called her a woman

and popped her bra in back. "You're my woman,"
I heard him say, and she slapped him. Visiting,
like I was, I felt shy. I listened to the newscaster
harder. He said how even though Marilyn
was beautiful and famous, no one had heard
her cry of loneliness that night. I saw how white-

blond her hair had been. "White
like that you call platinum," Jan said. "Women
do it with peroxide." I didn't care what else I heard—
I was thirteen, and my stomach hurt. Visiting
men overnight was Jan's idea! And Marilyn
Monroe was dead. Later Jan offered me castor

oil (they had peppermint-flavored castor
oil). I was terrified—they said I looked white—
was I still so upset about Marilyn
Monroe? But in the bathroom Jan said, "You're a woman,

now! You have a 'friend' visiting.
No wonder your stomach has been hurt-

ing. Did your mother tell you? Have you heard
of Tampax? That's what I use." She broadcast
my news all over that house I was visiting,
where I had to spend the night with an old white
sheet for rags. All night, in the womanly,
stuffed-fat underpants, I thought about Marilyn

and camping at the Shepherd of the Hills—white
water, with my dad flycasting, my womanly mother visiting
us in her yellow two-piece. "Here comes Marilyn Monroe!"

Fig

The fruit, uncooked, is pale green. It is shaped
like an old-fashioned hot-air balloon, veined with seams—
a surprise next to the fig preserves we used to have,
sugar-glazed, on Mama's foster mother's cut-glass dishes.

By then they looked like honey-colored roaches,
ugly but delicious. Dell was always right,
and not our favorite grandmother.
One day we disobeyed and tried them, early,

from her precious tree. In that strict lady's
Mississippi backyard, the grass was a yellow crew cut,
the ground a hot, plain place except for
that fig tree we weren't to climb or bother.

They didn't taste perfect, that raw.
They were milky. They made me think of words
like *nekked*, which is how it was spelled
in my mind—just how it sounded, out loud and bad.

I first bit into that plushy fruit
on my little sister's dare. The skin
was mottled like a lizard's, but then
the texture felt more like a tropical flower's

petals. The lip at the bottom was just where it would be
on a balloon. We sucked at those small paps, and I got
to liking my tongue on that blue-white squirting.
And so we'd play in Dell's dry garden.

A fig sounds right for Eden, too.
That tiny football would have made Eve more curious
than would a squat, everyday apple. A fig
would be easier to hide in a curled hand,

and stranger to taste, too amazing not to share.
This act was personal, so it made God mad. But a fig
is shameless with its wanton
shape, its opening, its rough and smooth and unknown

parts, wanting to show everything and be shown.

Rescuing My Sister

She'd climb the ladder in her pink bathing suit,
slight curve of tummy down to ruffled skirt,
jump holding her nose and screaming as she fell,
"Help! I'm drowning!" into her own whirlpool's

ring of bubbles. My cue to push off
from the rough, concrete side, to show my love,
hold my little sister in her sweet clamminess,
carry her by myself in this buoyant place.

You can carry a body in a swimming pool,
that realm as soft as Jell-O, until you hear a whistle
screech importantly, an arrow at your brilliant
game. Outside, dripping in the bleached-white scent

of the usual world, we saw the stuck-up, burned girls point,
learned we were weird. That pool was only meant
for boys who ducked each other, splashed us with cannonballs.
That was our segregated public pool: girls tanned with iodine, baby oil.

The Good China

Uncle Gene brought them back
from overseas: "Blue Willow"
dishes, with little landscapes
to think about while
you finished your milk
and the adults talked.

It was China, or Japan,
on the plates. The trees
were blue and beautifully
crooked, like the paths
up to the houses. The scene
invited you in, a zig-zag
route to a garden
on the handle of a cup, or up
past all houses,
to blue and white mountain air,
mysterious steps that stopped
at the high, sudden edge of a plate.

On top of each little world
was Sunday dinner: fried
chicken bones, grandmother's
mashed potatoes, forks
still scraping. Uncle Harold
was saying: "I've figured
something out. I know where hell
must be. It's down, right?
But too far down,
you'd be in China."
Uncle Harold had wanted to be
a missionary. Now he'd been reading,
in *Life Magazine*,

"speculations" about
the center of the earth.
"You know how hot
they say it is? How little
they've ever found out
about the place?"

He was chewing significantly.
Hell was true.
Aunt Maxine looked as pretty,
as bored, as usual. I had uncovered
a bridge over curvy waves,
a small, blue rainbow.

Hattiesburg

> after W.H. Auden's "Gare du Midi"

How odd that a direction—like South—
takes on meaning like a person's face.
After I had my half-Jewish children I contrived
ways never to return. Something about the mouth
of my grandfather I had seen sometimes. "A Town without Pity,"
sang Gene Pitney when I was twelve. A Wardian case
keeps curiosities, strange plants alive. We eluded that city,
hungry as a gingerbread house for my children to arrive.

How Girls Walk through the Eye of a Needle

The girls are getting slimmer now as if, perhaps,
to keep themselves from their mothers' fates.
They float in thin blouses above the fat plates,
their bodies forced like flowers into shape.
Not eating gives them a high window ledge
from which to contemplate life—an ascetic,
cloistered place. On the back pocket of jeans they like,
a tiny, red-inked Buddha smiles. "True Religion"
jeans are hard to get into, expensive and just
for the thinnest. I say, too loud, "It's like binding feet,"
embarrassing my daughter. But I did think
of those rich-girl feet that could not walk right—
at night they'd unwind the binding and the stink
drove husbands wild. Girls turn to bone so love will last.

Bloodletting

I've seen the cuts
on young girls' arms, the names of boys
on their wrists, near-misses with those veins
supposed to draw the dirty blue blood
away. Inside out, they trade the psyche's pain
for something more evident.

It's my own arm, anyway, someone thinks.
The famous violinist must wear
such flowing sleeves, even in summer.
After curtain calls, the curling iron
assures her that she is there. The wind
scissors her chest into windows
that flap like origami bird wings (open,
shut, tiny doors slamming
as if she were an empty house, paper-thin).

And so she holds the iron upon her arm
as she held the bow, before, to the violin,
and the scorching bite distracts—a rough lover's
reprimand, the reminding friction not so unlike
the tightened bow on the high-strung string.
This branding of her arm pilots
her air balloon of giddy bowing down
from that small, high stage where she hears
the helium cries from dressed-up strangers,
so thinly shrill she feels vertigo: "Encore!"

It is not suicide. The iron is a comforting
slap from a leading man: "Get a hold
of yourself," he'd say, in the ritzy room
with too many roses. Someone wants you.
Feel that, and that. It's what I saw in childhood,
almost took for a beauty mark.
Wives and housemaids sometimes wore

the prow-shaped burn, brown or rose,
of some mistake when they were ironing clothes.
Or a daisy-chain spattered on a thin, tanned forearm
from cooking the bacon too fast. The popular girls
wore shirts that showed their passion marks.
Those scars, worn like pins by the pretty girls,
might be some kind of scratching
on a door screen, thin as harmonics on a violin.
A little blood on the door, false or true,
can make the angel pass by.
Perhaps there is some way to make up
for one's luck? The opened windows
before a tornado, the vaccine, the letting
of a little poison in.

No, it is silly—and regretted, later, of course,
at the interview where one must wear sleeves to the wrist.
It is a response, but not the worst kind.
It is like getting a mother's pinch in church—
now I can cry and be mad instead
of being almost blown through
by the world's immense whirling.
And she will be sorry later, lifting me up to hug,
setting me back down again.

The casements rattle relentlessly
in the face of the vast, uncaring universe,
and so there is some relief to opening them,
as in the old belief in bloodletting—
that blood, itself, should be apologized for.
And so the barbers tried
to siphon out the body's mysterious surfeit,
wading in rivers for leeches
who could suck George Washington's illness dry.

Still, there are times when one small cut
feels natural, a pain that is separate and clean.
Blood flows. Water cuts
a mountain stream.

Paperback Rider

Something rustled around the edges
of my rich friend's spend-the-night parties,
at one of which I saw *Lady Chatterley's Lover*
in the living room, left in the bookcase by

her sophisticated parents, and so
I read about breasts swinging like bells
every chance I got when I was there
for our chapter of the "Beatles Fan Club,"

Susan Moncrief naming John the sexiest,
us pretending the Beatles were coming over—
"Let's play you're Paul and I'm Jane
Asher," someone would say—so we had

our own "hard day's nights" together,
dressing up in ties and vests like
the long-haired girlfriends in the pictures,
taking turns being Beatles

and singing, fondling and winking,
though someone's kid sister was George a lot
and chose me, whispered "luv" and "bird"
in my ear, put her arm around me,

was good at sounding gruff and Liverpudlian—
"his voice grew husky," I thought,
remembering what I'd read in some books—
and we didn't even know how excited we were,

our blood rushing to new places,
me thinking one song was "Paperback Rider"
at first, not "Writer." Well, in that atmosphere
Susan was transformed—she was all right,

not sick ever again—you can think that for a while
and it couldn't be true, what I'd heard,
fluttering like leaves in the wind or
the dog-eared, ruthless flapping of

the cheap pages in an adult's book
that gives you a stomachache to read
but then it's too late—
too far, too much, too bad to be true

so why did we want to hear the rumor
it must have been, the kind that spreads,
when she came in, new, at our school?
See that girl? She's going to die.

Her parents are keeping it a secret from her.
She has too many white blood cells.
That's when I saw her, pale and tragic,
remote and a little fat, not from food

but from air, like she could float
already. She had long, straight, dark-brown hair
and saved us from our fear and pity by
inviting us over in a stuck-up, careless voice.

After I moved I found out she did die.
Some girl sent a telegram that said "PASSED AWAY."
I fell on the kitchen floor, crying.
"She was just seventeen," sang

The Beatles. Mama was mad.
Why did that stupid girl have to send that?
"Try not to dwell on it, honey."
I'd say that to my daughter, too—

Daddy's getting better, I'd say,
which is only likely from a distance.
I remember that house, how cool
her parents were. I never heard them yell.

Her mom threw parties for us and just disappeared.
Her dad worked as a photographer
for the *Hattiesburg American*. That burned-out store
of the murdered businessman, the trial

of the Klansman they caught, Cecil Sessum,
gripping onto his fat mother, Velma.
Her gaze at the camera is the hardest
you've ever seen.

He took her picture
in the Mississippi light. What does it matter
what other parents think?
Let little girls read dirty books all night.

June 1969

after Kenneth Koch's "You Were Wearing"

You were always carrying *The Way of Zen*
in the back pocket of your Levi's,
and we were drinking Gallo Burgundy when
you couldn't believe I hadn't heard
of Vincent Van Gogh, and Mother drove you
up the switchbacks, around the curves,
in her big old Thunderbird with the bad brakes,
up past Lake Lure to Penland,
where you met Paulus Berensohn, the potter,
whose friend was M.C. Richards, who wrote
Centering. Things were happening for you,
but my mother is the one who set things spinning
like a 45 record on the spindle—taking
your talent seriously and researching Penland
the way she used to find out about
music schools for my prodigy sister,
and Penland (and your penis, my mother said later)
led to all those rich friends from Esalen,
Nathalie Murphy giving you sixty acres
if you'd live on her place on the mountain between Ukiah
and Mendocino, but you wanted me as part
of the deal, so we drove up to her paradise
for a while, me skinny dipping with you and her
that first day to prove what I never did prove.
I picked up that book by Alan Watts
in her living room. "No, you're not at a place yet
to get this." That's when she gave me
what looked like a fat comic book for kids,
Be Here Now by Baba Ram Dass,
and everyone but me had a Coors beer.

First Love

Mama, you were my first love.
From you I learned what a body is for,
skin against skin, that mystery.
You were so different from me.

From you I learned what a body's
for—to be rocked and sung to—
you were so different from me
and sang that song you made up.

To be rocked and sung to
and later to sing to someone else.
You sang that song you made up,
"Baby, baby my darling now don't…"

I could sing to someone else
but I only remember parts—"Don't cry,
Baby, baby, my darling, now don't…"
and something like "stars in the sky."

I only remember parts. "Don't cry."
The melody was brilliant and soothing,
something like stars in the sky.
I've tried to sing it to my children,

the brilliant, soothing melody.
It wasn't just any lullaby
and I've tried to sing it to my children.
You were too carefree to write it down.

It wasn't just any lullaby.
I can almost hear it when I'm crying,
what you were too free to write down.
That missing part, that harmony,

I can almost hear it when I'm crying.
Although it came to mean nothing,
that missing and that harmony.
Why must our feelings change?

Although it came to mean nothing,
my first lover was a Taurus like you
and there are feelings that must change
between a girl and a mother.

My first lover was a Taurus like you—
both stubborn, both earthy and beautiful.
Between a girl and her mother
things can be so very close.

You were both stubborn and beautiful.
One night we were all drunk with Gallo
(how things can be so very close)
and you kissed me with your tongue.

One night we were drunk on Gallo wine
and I knew he was your lover too.
You kissed me the way dogs piss on lawns,
and I got over it all, I thought.

I knew he was your lover too.
Outside I saw The Big Dipper.
I got over it all, I thought,
until I had children of my own.

I went outside to see the constellations.
Mama, you were my first love
and now I have children of my own.
Skin against skin, that mystery.

First Marriage

After the wedding his fist flew, connected.
My face was bruised. It caught us by surprise,
that " sudden blow," as in the Yeats sonnet
I had to write a paper on for class.

My eye was bruising. We were both surprised.
He'd never touched me that way before.
I still had to write the paper for my class.
He hit me like his father hit his mother.

He'd never touched me that way before,
but he'd seen it as a boy. I couldn't concentrate.
He hit me like his father used to hit his mother,
and we were that old pattern, pitiful and trite.

He'd seen it as a boy. How could I concentrate
on Yeats's question, far away as a Grecian vase?
My husband had become his father, another wife-beater.
He cried and brought me ice for my face.

That question—circular as a Grecian vase—
soothes like music, like a healing balm.
My young husband cried, brought me ice for my face.
I stopped crying before he did. You have to stay calm.

It soothed like music, healing like a balm,
and I covered my bruises with make-up.
I stopped crying. You have to stay calm.
I studied the poem—"Being so caught up..."

I put on my Cover Girl concealer too thick—
while Leda "put on his knowledge with his power."
I wrote the paper. I had to get caught up
with the class. My professor asked, *Is something the matter?*

Here's what you can learn from a man's powerful
fist: Pretend you're okay. Say it's no big thing.
Guilt just riles them up again. Smile, say it doesn't matter.
Yeats's sonnet made "being mastered" sound thrilling.

I'll bet Leda didn't say a thing,
lying in that "white rush" until he was finished
and dropped her. Yeats made rape sound thrilling.
Everything connects. That swan, his fist.

Ship in a Bottle

It takes such fine work, making your escape.
It is the raising of a miniature, secret ship
inside a bottle, pulling it up with thread,
trying not to injure, trying not to make the child.
He used to punch back when that old cowhand
beat his mommy up. In psych class we learned
the trait gets handed down. My IUD fell out, useless little
helmet—like a horseshoe crab with a tail.
The self-righteous couple walked from next door:
We heard screaming, Sunday. Is that a black eye?
Soon I would wriggle out—as from under the covers
when someone removes his muscled arm, turns over.
I'm sure, when she kept delaying, Penelope
was desperate. I let mine die—small suitors.

The Exact Coordinates of Hell

Mama, dying, saw Hell on the hospital wall.
It flickered like an old home movie—
Why, there it is, she said, staring, like a child,
past the foot of the bed, and people pretended
to look as they look for a spider you're afraid of
before they tell you it's just a nail hole.
My father was frightened enough to get her to sing
"The Old Rugged Cross," and it hurt to imagine
her humbled enough to join in, bowing her head—
the wild pianist caught by the choir minister.
It was Beethoven she loved,
and she could play the hell out of the Widor
Toccata on the organ (which sounds like
Rachmaninoff and the Rolling Stones taking over
the plainness of a white Baptist church).
And she'd hurt me too, so my heart
fell asleep like your feet when you sit too long.
When her breathing slowed and sounded like drowning,
the bored nurse said, *They don't even feel it*
by this point.   Later I realized
the meaning of that scene on the wall.
She'd lied to her kids so we wouldn't know,
saying "polio," covering her scars with long skirts.
And then, one day, she'd told my handsome
boyfriend, not me, the story. Tuberculosis
of the hip, they called it then, that disease Annie Sullivan's
little brother had. She got this because her stepfather,
the sailor, wild with whiskey and murdering
her mother, must have thrown her into the fireplace
like a little rag. Oh, my mother,
my little Cinderella,
you had already had your punishment
and were just remembering, trailing clouds
from the ingle, that miniature Manderley.
Hell was the size of a dollhouse that day.

The True Story

(based on a photograph found near New Orleans;
my grandmother and ladies in front of a church)

*For a figure see that you have full light, full shade; all the rest
will come naturally; it often amounts to very little.*
—Manet

Beautiful eyes like that come from either
childbirth or anemia. She looks like my mother,
who plays the organ and doesn't believe in God.

But this is an old picture—
no place for colors more than ochre, or for us.
My mother isn't sure of her mother's first name.
She overheard the gossip one time.

Mama was a few weeks old. An older lady,
amazing as a witch, was the neighbor
who came to visit and found them.
Maybe her soul is a glint,
morning's light on one tree in the pine woods.

This is the kind of story—
what we have of it—that sounds too much
like the stories I used to read, at ten,
at the beauty parlor: *True
Confessions* and *Photoplay*.

But there are shadows underneath her eyes.
They curve out blue and wrong for this shot.
You forget that it's noon in the picture with no shade,
that this is already over with. You can imagine
the wisteria, and wading down Little Buffalo Creek
with your skirts up—shrill of ice water
halfway up your legs and the sharp rocks,
and muddy crawfish—you can imagine
how things must have happened.

She frowns for this Sunday
picture-taking. Her breasts
and the way she slumps one shoulder
would keep you from guessing she's thirteen.
She's married to the minister,
and one of his children, calling her "Mama,"
is older than she is.

When the minister dies, next year
on the barber's table,
the girl in this picture
will be pregnant with my mother and rich—
golden hills way beyond her window.
With the sun so hot,
and just the older ladies to talk to,
this girl might rather lie outside
on warm, prickly, yellow grass,
drink iced tea with sugar in it.

Her mouth frowns; her eyes bloom regardless.
Perhaps the sailor
is walking there already.
He'll smile.
Her land will vanish for that smile.
One day this new husband
will drink the last whiskey
and throw her baby onto hot hearthstones.

You can see how things don't fit:
her in this old, stern picture.
She's too young—and too familiar.
Hope burns through this Sunday frame
like a red garter.

Her eyes are as stupid as magnolias.
She drifts into getting murdered when she's fifteen
the way a day is the wrong day and it rains.

This was so deep into Mississippi
they never could catch the man.
But you can see, in this picture,
how people are related.
They'll have their mother's knees,
or eyes, in spite of everything.

II

Mysterious Barricades

François Couperin must have loved some girl
and known how to argue, how to twine fingers
in a dance—how one idea will break onto another
like waves that rear and kneel, how the sea's curls must rise
in time to the moon, how a girl can kiss back.

This is what you hear in music that turns
with the steadiness of a merry-go-round,
the ornate horses ready to burst from their glass
bodies and race each other across a hill
in their real shapes—they are that excited,
ready to bolt except for this composition
the composer called "mysterious barricades,"
this maze with turnings through a trimmed
suspense: the coy vistas of old boxwood,
this fond and winding argument designed to hold
a loved one fast and keep those horses,
those good horses, from galloping away.

My Life at the Convenience Store

Today I almost blew myself up,
me and this old panhandler
who reminds me of the man
in Anna Karenina's dream.

Me and this old panhandler—
we were drenched in gasoline.
In Anna Karenina's dream
the man's always there by the train.

We were drenched in gasoline—
the hose was coiling like a snake.
He's always there by the train,
the man making her feel doomed.

The hose was coiling like a snake.
It was like kids playing with a sprinkler.
The man made me feel doomed,
and his pants and shoes were soaked.

It was like kids playing with a sprinkler
but this wasn't water and he wanted change.
His pants and shoes were soaked,
and we were yelling to those inside

"We need water!" And he wanted change.
Then this woman drove up with a cigarette,
if you can believe it. My skirt was wet
and we were yelling to those inside

and this woman drives up with a cigarette!
I walked to her car and asked her to move it,
if you can believe it, with my skirt wet.
Then I ran inside and screamed for water

after I'd walked to her car and asked her to move it.
It's always like a short story there anyway.
I ran inside and screamed for water
and a line of people just looked at me.

It's always like a short story there anyway.
I said I'd almost killed him and we needed water.
The line of people just looked at me.
I announced I'd given him five dollars.

I said I'd almost killed him and we needed water.
Some man finally said how it evaporates fast.
After I announced I'd given the man five dollars,
"Oh, that's Panama!" someone said.

Some man said how it evaporates fast
and I shouldn't be so worried.
"Oh, that Panama!" someone said,
"was he bothering you, honey?"

I shouldn't be so worried.
"Go on, Panama, you've made your money!"
"Was he bothering you, honey?"
Some other guy thanked me for the excitement.

"Go on, Panama, you've made your money!
He's always around here, pestering people."
Some other guy thanked me for the excitement
and a nice woman went out and yelled at Panama.

He's always around there, pestering people,
and he's said things to me before.
A nice woman went out and yelled at Panama.
"Tell your husband you need to get married,"

he's said to me, things like that, before.
But today I almost blew myself up.
"Tell your husband you need to get married!"
He reminds me of the dream in *Anna Karenina*.

Party Float

There was that view of the river and also the bed
like a party float, the kind with skirts that echo
the skirts of the homecoming court's dresses.
The room seemed built for love more than hotel
rooms maybe should be, all the ironed pillowcases
and there were so many pillows carefully

arranged as if we were company carefully
chosen as good lovers, people right for a bed,
finally, all night—washed feet, kisses,
the feeling of being tucked in as if sex echoes
innocence, the child's first vacation hotel.
The longed-for feeling of waking up undressed

within such range of the other, undressed,
and just as ready to touch back, carefully
or not, whatever you want and want to tell
met by equal liking for that in the bed
so wide it might have floated, echoed
to swan boats outside the windows bolted in case—

too bad, I thought, they didn't open. And in our case—
your Bleak House divorce, your need to undress
but not talk. Enjoy the moment, you said. I echoed
myself, you stared at the river carefully
as Narcissus and, really, that lovely, wanted bed
did us no good, though someone from the hotel

knocked: *did we want service?* She handed me hotel
towels and I thought of narrow beds where we had kissed
before. I gave her a five and she smiled at me. That wide bed
didn't need to be remade. We'd undressed
in the perfect place where we could be careless,
your not wanting to "hash over things" echoing

back from the pool where we sat one night, echoing
off of me who wished to hash over things. That hotel—
that expensive paradise—we couldn't have cared less.
By the time we got there we didn't wish to kiss.
You went out to dinner, tired and beautifully dressed;
I had gin and tonics on the homecoming bed.

A "Catch 22," you said. That float of a bed,
that hotel that echoed like an aria—we cared less
when at last we arrived. We hardly kissed, undressed.

Orpheus and Eurydice at the AWP

"Just to see," we went to hell and back.
It was Austin, Texas—palm trees and a view,
a pilgrimage of bats. We saw the bridge and those dark

tea-trays up from Mexico way, soaring over oar strokes
of rowing teams sliding by in the blue
dusk. Naturally Orpheus let her slip back—

a man can't help but take another look.
Could he trust her and was she really true?
The female bats make it every year to the bridge's dark,

flying by ear like a Bach invention or the music
of Jimi Hendrix, that sad song "Hey Joe."
All we did was sightsee and then go back.

You said you felt "torn." I called you a jerk,
myself a fool. Our hotel window showed a blue
concert, bats flying to and from the bridge in the dark

in perfect swoons of fidelity. Your face had this look
as if I really might not follow you.
I felt crazy, seeing that bridge in the dark.
I'd stay in hell, just to want you back.

That Poem about Your Ex's Breasts

to J.D.

Why does the word have to sound like "guzzle"?
Why not take the beautiful sound, "gazelle"?

Guzzling white wine, you wrote about her nipples,
in a marvelous, dancing, resounding ghazal

which works in English just fine.
It makes me jealous, your astounding ghazal.

I can hear you nuzzling and sucking her nipples.
You write it so naturally, that confounded ghazal.

I must hold the banister as I step down.
I need enjambment, the bound of the gazelle.

Mine are the best, you say, now, as you gaze,
but unfortunately, I found that youthful ghazal,

couplets about smuggling her into your hotel,
wine on her nipples that you tongued in the ghazal.

Her published nipples reappeared in an anthology:
two pressed rosehips bound in a book of ghazals.

You'd come too soon when you were young, you said.
The ghazal is the hunt and the sound of the gazelle

when it is too late. The song is a kind of enclosure,
a little music box, a room in Paris bounded by a ghazal.

Two-Part Invention

Bach's on, and so when you take
my fingers and place them like you want
on you, I remember my mother teaching me
piano, my hand resting in hers, my fingers
gently placed on this note and that one—
how good that felt, like my hand going on
a little ride, how I liked the feeling of my fingers
being spread, pulled and pushed just gently,
a soothing massage to show my hand
the right position for a chord.

And that's how we did it today,
with Bach on and light through the window,
because we are still teaching each other.

Trying to Write a Love Poem for You, I Write about the Father of My Children

We rearrange our histories and think,
if you had not been married then or if
she'd stayed in Provincetown and we had been
alone by my car, how far would you have gone?
And I was in a playing mood, bereaved.

We rub and knock the possibilities
like scrabble tiles and try to form a word
for what we want. No word like this exists,
nor world, with the same children happier.
No one had lost a father. This would mean
no Oak Ridge, Tennessee, no radio-
active dimes in the machine, which I
can almost feel just how he thumbed—cold,
silvery, beyond all time or wishing.

On Being Alive at the Same Time

The operas change the ending—make it okay
that Orpheus looked back. Nobody can stand
this—the way she really was following
at first, how ordinary their walk
could have been. The amazing thing—
her being there was as true
as last week, when they were almost bored.

We were holding gin and tonics on our knees.
There was an interruption
in the programming—a plane crash, people
wanting their lives. For a minute
we saw like Orpheus.
They were like us.

Those people accepted the Potomac.
Long ago we refreshed
our gin and tonics,
went back to *The Thin Man* on t.v.
The groaning plane was settling in,
becoming permanent, like the silver dollar.

We were all alive at the same time, then.
And that is too hard to keep
your mind on, but I saw, on television,
the flimsy difference death is,
that man in the cold river, his bald head bobbing
while he treads water, the camera zooming in.
Halfway out of the icy water, he acts
like himself again, makes gestures
that are second nature, like opening a door
for a girl. He helps a stewardess
grab for the rope, and then she is swinging

from the helicopter, home free.
And he is yelling to the pilot
like he'd talk with a friend
over fishing poles—ordinary words
of men on the same side of a stream
until the pilot, returning, finds the man
gone—this man who had his chance back,
firm as the features on his face.

Falling All Those Stories Down

(remembering, ten years later)

Imagine the kind of love,
the instant-coffee marriage,
that fastness of vows
some could give each other

to jump from the high window
together, holding hands.
Those are stories we can almost bear,
people flying down the towers,

falling with the debris,
lucky enough to lock arms
so in twos or threes
they fell like angels.

Unbearable to watch how some flew
alone, turned upside-down like
a paper doll or a toy sailboat in a bathtub.
Unbearable to think of the ones inside.

The ones who jumped
had to leave the burning others
whose pain I have no right
to speak of—whose stories

are as far away as stars.
But some of you gripped hands,
while all those stories were burning
down, you held fast to a strange hand.

It was anyone's hand, and now
the strangest love,
the quickest love of saying *Jump with me
and be the one who understands my life.*

Widow's Walk: An Apology for Vampires

> But my very feelings changed to repulsion and terror when I saw the whole man slowly emerge from the window and begin to crawl down the castle wall over that dreadful abyss, face down . . . move downwards with considerable speed, just as a lizard moves along a wall.
> —from Jonathan Harker's journal,
> *Dracula*, Bram Stoker

When you're too close to a death, people are appalled
you would want to go on living. A famous poet confided
he was already in bed with someone else
an hour after his wife died. So what, I say.
He was trying to tell you something about grief.

Now that my husband's dead I've been wondered at
by people I'd trusted not to disapprove.
But think of the heroines in Bram Stoker's *Dracula*—
pinned-down butterflies for his own, Victorian
predilections—they had to wear the smothering
garlic necklaces to bed, their nightgowns buttoned
up to the throat; the windows, of course, had to be shut.
To be good they couldn't be sexy. The nicest girl
was a mousy stenographer, and even she
had to be saved from herself.

Interesting, isn't it, how he made them all get kissed
by the lizard? For that is just how Dracula looked, at night—
not flying, like in the movies, but climbing gingerly out
of his window upside-down, face to his mansion's wall,
all for his ache to meet new blood.

Once a girl got kissed, the symptoms were odd.
She was at once more vivacious
and weaker. Her mouth and cheeks were as red
as if she were wearing the most tasteless, drugstore brand
of lipstick. And yet she tired easily. She was moody.
Really, she was like a teenager on her period.

Why was Mr. Stoker so interested in this? Why did he make
such a horror show of desire? Surely he'd felt it, himself.
Which brings me back to the grief, and why
it makes perfect sense that those girls, once kissed,
would crave the kissing, shock their inexperienced, blond
fiancés. And why, when someone's life has taken
that awful, legendary, downward turn,
she might well wish to crawl like a lizard
and face the wall for love.

Demeter's Escape

Ice numbs the pain, and moving around
jostles the sore heart. Why should we blame
Demeter for, allegedly, making the world cold?
Nothing like an icy martini.

Demeter's sore heart could not bear the jostling.
I thought of the speed bumps when my water broke,
but these shocks played in a new key. No martini
would fix this pain. We drink anyway.

My husband drove me carefully to the hospital that day.
On the night the eye specialist could not say
this thing could be fixed, we went out to drink.
A thrill the other side of being in labor.

The night the specialist kept us so long
we went to our old haunt, La Rosa's, with our kids.
This was the opposite sort of contraction,
like my sickness in the schoolyard, waiting for my dad.

La Rosa's had been remodeled, all imitation wood.
Just new things, now, and no returning,
like my sickness in the schoolyard, the last kid on the swings.
I blushed in the waiting room where my kids were good,

where I learned this news, this end of seasons,
as if I were ashamed. Some hot spotlight on my face
while my children looked at books and were good.
I held onto the stem of my martini.

At the worst luck, why do we feel ashamed?
I confided to the server how the doctor wasn't sure,
just to explain my second gin straight up with olives.
My kids were drawing with crayons on their menus.

The server was kind, sure we'd get better news.
The drink came with olives on a toothpick sword.
I loved art deco, "atomic" martini glasses.
My kids played knights with the tiny swords.

You can sip a martini, feel cool like in *The Thin Man*.
Demeter's pain cools the world now and then.
En garde! my children said. Then we went to "Johnny's Toys."
Pain always has such different, sharp-pointed shapes.

Demeter's pain cools the world now and then.
The doctor said tumors can cause color-blindness.
Pain is an assortment of sharp-pointed edges.
En garde! said Tess and Jason. They saw the "super balls."

The doctor was perplexed by their daddy's color-blindness.
No wonder Demeter blurred the air with crystals.
Those new super balls bounced in every direction.
Imagine a world which is warmer, faster.

No wonder Demeter blurred the air with crystals.
When water heats, the bubbles come faster and faster.
Imagine a world which is ever warmer, faster.
There are times we can't bear to think of.

When water heats, the bubbles rise faster.
Every day is new and won't be returning.
Demeter made winter for the unbearable times.
She would just sleep while her girl was away.

Every day is new and won't be returning.
My husband had a tumor in his brain.
For a few years all I did was sleep, drink cold martinis.
I'd go back to bed after taking my children to school.

Lost Painting

> *the jolly great truth that it is art alone*
> *that triumphs over fate.*
> —Henry James

I saw it years ago—the painting
of a cocktail party at your father's house.
The oblique and disappearing
shape of a party, people
edging in and out
in creams and browns and pinks,
and the exaggerated v-shaped
quality of that time—triangle
of piano and the low-cut v's of dresses,
a *v* on the stem of a martini glass,
those crazy, boomerang
ash trays in olive green, high heels
modeled after the Bridge of Sighs,
arches which formed, in negative space,
upside-down triangles, tiny Gothic windows
opening onto Oriental blue in the woven rug.

That was how parties went at your house
when your mother was alive. So the painting implied
her existence. The door to the kitchen,
that yellow rectangle near the edge of the painting,
signified her behind it, surrounded by a good third
of the guests wandering off the canvas to see her,
share a cigarette, help her arrange
desserts on a plate. Your mother,
Mrs. Dalloway in Oak Ridge,
married to the head of the National Lab,
died not long after that—
the caterer of the new wife's parties
had been her closest friend.

The painting should have been
in a museum. By the time I knew you
it was hanging in the basement
overlooking the ping-pong table,
an interesting kind of hell for physicists.
Absurd, I thought, that this good time made, perhaps,
less mortal by the painter and given to your mother
had been denied its proper place.
The new wife had "a real Picasso"
for the place above the mantel upstairs:
a clown face, a primary-color splash
that squatted on its throne above the fireplace.

I imagined the painting in our apartment,
that souvenir from the Atomic Age,
a party that no longer could exist.
I wanted it for the same bad reasons
your stepmother must have wanted the Picasso.
I asked you to ask your Pop for the painting.

But you didn't feel "comfortable" asking.
Something stubborn—heavy as a doorstop—
kept you from telling him
That was my mother's painting.
Later on, I got you to call him up and ask.
By that time, of course, it had vanished.
Your dad wasn't even sure
which painting we meant. He said
he'd ask his wife—she'd look.

I hope she gave it away and didn't
throw it in the trash. Maybe someone saw it
and it hangs in some other room,
and in this room the partiers are anonymous,

no one knows who they were.
They are well enough drawn, though,
to remind the people who saved it
of other gatherings. The "*v*" which repeats
in the glasses, in the art-deco form
of the painting—it flew somewhere
like the v-shaped bravery of birds,
some of whom must drop out,
and then the birds find their shape again,
go on winging to their promised land.

III

Unmade Bed

> after Sargent's *An Artist in His Studio*, also titled
> *No Nonsense*

White is not white unless we see
a crease of blue. Unless the bed, unmade,
reveals the loops of shadow, terraces
of cools and greens that off-set abstract heights,
the once high-flown feather pillow. White is that glare
so Medusa-pure we can't look at it without
deflecting that glance with a mirror.
Light is celestial, spun-glass we used to call
angel hair placed on the mantel. It pierces like
a spinning wheel, dares Prometheus to rock-climb,
John Singer Sargent to expose this borrowed bedroom
to an audience. Light is the odalisque
on a messy, narrow bed—its fan dance of shades,
intensities, hints, garlands
of swig and swag. The crumpled, contrapuntal
counterpane's a waterfall down to the blues,
a chromatic fantasy, dropped wallet open on a street,
unfolding, unbuttoning. See the bleached linen's undone
hospital corners, the loosening, scooting,
the scumbling brushwork, the snake
of wrinkling sheet, the fiction good as sunlight.

Sun on the unmade bed is the artist's self-portrait,
showing three painstaking paintings:
the landscape his friend paints on his easel;
the one just drying on that bed, about to mark
the bed itself with paint;
the larger canvas encompassing those blue
and emerald jewels.
The center of this work is itself,
the exercise involved invoking light,
the vertiginous, tiring scaling of some peak,
a pianist practicing Hanon's climbing scales—

my sister's chore as mine was to wash the dishes—
suffice it to say there are so many variations possible
on the subject of emptiness or the absence
of color, such nuances under our particular
sun. The bed's tangled sheets, indigo
and cream, show arabesques of near and far,
the painter sitting sideways so we see his balding head,
that curve of naked shine, Sargent's signature.

Brake, Brake, Brake, Ephemeral Car

> on Jane Freilicher's painting, *The Car*

Almost abstract, stopped just short of heartbreak,
the car is a blue ellipse on the chrome-yellow marsh.
We cannot tell its particular make, as a flower
or a figure of blue in a Bonnard stays blurred forever.

We see the ellipse of a plate or a face as part
of this harmony of breakfast. Someone from outside
leans a plump arm on the open Dutch door for no
particular reason. *Luxe, calme et volupté*, said Baudelaire.

That harmony of breakfast is what friends have
for a while. Jane would say that the coffee was on,
and they all found her adorable, voluptuous and calm.
When she got engaged, Larry Rivers slit his wrists.

John, Kenneth, Larry, I have the coffee set.
In an interview Rivers spoke of her as just "some girl."
Fairfield Porter's portrait shows him with bandaged wrists.
She's Jane Freilicher, actually. She's now married to another man.

In an interview Rivers spoke of her as just "some girl"
who inspired him to change from music to painting.
Is she still painting? Who is it? But this was actually
Jane, who, for her part, mentioned Larry's being a "skirt-chaser."

She inspired this whole group. The gay men loved her too.
That car parked recklessly, everyone going "Chez Jane,"
the New York School of Poets with skirt-chaser.
She was their amused muse, and wrote, with Kenneth Koch, a poem

about that car, the one parked recklessly in this painting.
The line I like—*Dashboard: I am my setting sun, a dashboard*—
I'll bet it's hers. And then Kenneth Koch, messing with Tennyson
when he wrote the line—*Brake, brake, brake!*

The dashboard's voice fits the car on the marsh—a setting sun,
an arc, ellipse of blue moon explaining the marsh.
They collaborated, they jazzed up Tennyson's "Break, Break, Break."
John Ashbery wrote from Paris that she had to read Proust.

As in "ellipsis," the oval elides details on that marsh—
as in another car, the dune buggy that ran over Frank O'Hara.
The postcard from France was about the "ephemeral and casual."
Frank O'Hara wrote a *calligramme*—words in the shape of her face—

and a dune buggy ran over him on Fire Island,
a scenario you'd imagine in one of his poems.
The lines were beautiful—a drawing, a concrete poem.
And then he was killed by another concrete thing.

He imagined other scenarios—he and Jane in a canoe.
Arabesque hood, hint of fins…the ellipse might be a Studebaker.
Frank O'Hara died in such a slapdash, Thomas Hardy way.
The brushstrokes of the car rhyme softly with the reeds.

That ellipse might be a Studebaker…arabesque hood, idea of fins…
but the marsh is a tablecloth, the car a vase of flowers,
empathizing with the blowing marsh reeds.
John Ashbery wrote about Proust's madeleines.

The marsh is the tablecloth, the car a vase of blue marguerites.
My friend Dianne and I would sit on her porch in Charlotte.
Ashbery shared Proust's madeleines with Jane.
We'd eat tomato sandwiches and pecan sandies.

In college, one night, we hitched a ride to the last SDS convention
with the creative-writing professor I had a crush on.
We'd have instant coffee like writers on her porch in Charlotte.
That might be why I love Jane Freilicher's painting.

We're old and we don't speak. We broke each other's hearts.
But look at Jane's painting of that car on the marsh,
painted in all its casual, ephemeral being.
It was true because it was passing, that day.

Short Story Based on a David Hockney Painting

We're above sea-level,
at Mount Olympus height,
the surrounding mountains like a high English hedge
of topiary cones—greens, blues and violets—
which frame the expensive privacy. Full sun
on the pool so there must be that thrill, that cocktail mix
of cool air and bright sun on the skin at once.
Of course, for us, it is still a picture we can't step into.
This vista, though, almost makes you feel the sunlight
or remember it when you were twelve.
The image is not beige and slick, like a magazine picture
of someone else's wealth. Sometimes a painting
can soothe us like the water. No one needs a swimsuit
at the free museum.

And, besides, there's something juicy here—
we're let in on what's wrong—all happy families are alike,
Tolstoy begins, and isn't this the truth here?
The flaws, the curves, the story of the painting—it's all laid out
for us to bask in. Even the pool is a comic,
the water abstract-expressionist—soft-edged,
cartoon diamonds, impossible as clouds,
blue bleeding blue and white lollipop swirls,
signature Hockney way to look at water.

The conflict is between the two men.
It is either dull marriage or an affair.
There is the hunk in the pool, broad-shouldered,
tan, but also wavy and ephemeral, swimming underwater, holding
his breath in his abstract-expressionist, beautiful body,
his body which is one with the water, gorgeously ignoring
his overdressed audience. The artist, as bone-dry as the museum-goer,

shows he's outside another frame—the pool.
The painter stands on the warm concrete in his shoes and socks,
in his white linen pants, blue shadows in the wrinkles,
in his flame-colored jacket.
He is peering down at the swimmer.

Narcissus is in the water,
and he is not drowning. He is eternally swimming.
He's just fine. The man standing, seeing only his love—
his petulance, his ego, his lateness for dinner—
he is leashed to this imperviousness, enchanted.
He would never see his own reflection
in this opaque, glossy pool. But he will paint
this stubborn moment,
its rippling blues echoing
to guests at his beautiful pool.

Ode to de Kooning's Penis

after Marot's Blason du Beau Tétin

I liked the sound, and men have often taken parts
to mean the whole. Also, frankly, your portraits
made me mad in the museum. Those women stick
their tongues and nipples out in such a frenzy,
peering out from gilded frames like they could smash
right through. I felt hated, myself, and chilled,

seeing my sex as your canvas. Little Dutch child,
always you return to these broken parts.
I know your mother would come home smashed.
You used her shoes as boats. The portraits,
goes one theory, were how you got to stick
it back to her. I thought of Hitchcock's *Frenzy*,

his film that shows too much. In *Frenzy*,
the detective is amusingly chilled
by his wife's cuisine. Her breadsticks
snap like the lady's fingers did. The part
the wife plays in her sexy apron is the portrait
of another fool, the woman found, smashed

inside a potato delivery van. Smashing,
she'd teased the man to his stickpin frenzy.
This, too, suggests the self-portrait—
his mum and dad's practical joke on their child,
laughing with the cops. So the woman's parts
are showing. The necktie makes her tongue stick

out and that makes it worse, the slapstick.
Abstract expressionists liked getting smashed
so much your wife called it all "a ten-year party."
At the Cedar everyone was drunk and in a frenzy.
That girl in the car had just escaped the war. Childish,
Pollock drank, drove faster, said your figures betrayed

art. Sometimes it was Elaine's face. Her self-portrait
shows a glimmer of how you two could stick.
Arabesque of ash tray. Green, green vase. A child
despairs for order while the gods are smashing
a blue delft sky. You two were in a frenzy.
She liked how men's clothes cut them into two parts.

She got stuck while painting Kennedy's portrait. Frenzy
leaves us chilled. He posed for her in Florida, in shirtsleeves.
Elaine looked smashing in her halter top. Did he notice that part?

The Girl Taking Jackson Pollock's Picture

> After a photograph of Jackson Pollock and Ruth Kligman, taken on the day of Pollock's fatal car crash. This poem is an elegy to an absence—the other fatally wounded person in the car, Edith Metzger, the photographer.

My subjects are hefty and rounded,
substantial as Cezanne apples
except in black and white.
They are full of "joie de vivre,"
plump, arms and legs entangled
as in that painting of people dancing
by Matisse, holding hands in a circle,
that I might have seen at an exhibition
when I was so young my papa carried me
everywhere. We met Hermann Goering
at the museum. Not long after, my father stood
in the long line for our visas.

Now these two wrestle and cavort
while I look on. She has thrust her camera at me,
wants me to take their picture.
His stomach laps over the belt to his trousers
that are speckled with paint. In just her black bathing suit
she straddles his leg; he grips her soft thigh in his hands.

I told her I'd love to meet Jackson Pollock,
and it's true, I was flattered she asked me
for the weekend. It is not what I expected.
I feel sick when he comes too close
or winks at me. For breakfast he had beer.
He drove us from the train too fast,
made his tires squeal on every curve.
Then they disappeared
into the bedroom, let me hear
Oh my God! Oh, Jesus!

I wasn't shocked or offended.
But I have been surprised, over and over,
by the reach of America's landscape,
its headlong, furious grasp at life,
captured in these new paintings
which take up so much space and air.
The house, outrageously sparse,
two bentwood rocking chairs placed
so the arms vaguely gesture toward the water,
the feel of my bare feet on floor planks rubbed
to a gloss, no splinters anywhere.
Just imagine living here!

At the barn, which is his studio,
I saw the window still smashed
from when he'd misplaced his key;
the glass shards gave his paintings
a glitter that seemed reflective.

When we stepped inside I let myself go,
got so upset and melodramatic
I think I am becoming American.
Still, I dread that soiree down the road
a friend of his is giving.

In the barn I spilled our terrible story
which gets transformed when it's told
into something sensational and slippery.
In this land it echoes with the twang
of a tall tale. But no one can bear
hearing too much of another's sorrows.
I knew, as I was speaking,
that I sounded too shrill, off-key.

She was crying about him never leaving
his wife and so I said yes. I really came here
to be at the beach. I love the surf and how it sounds,
the ocean washing up and then back over the stones
like an old laundry maid scrubs clothes
on a riddled washboard.
And the light reminds me,
in its whimsy of bright and dark,
of light shining through window shutters—
as in some Vermeer being sold
for safe passage here.

I'm taking you girls to that party, he said.
He likes to drive in his green Oldsmobile
convertible with the top down.
By now I'm sure we will hardly have time
to lie around in the sun
and I wanted to get a little tan
for the beauty parlor where I answer
the phone. Now we live in the Bronx.
My mother and little brother and I
have a safe little nest of sorts.
Boring, too—no one sees you as
you really are. At that party tonight
I'll be snubbed, ignored.

I could bury myself
in this soft sand I feel between my toes,
hear the seagulls and a thunder of pure
saltwater. The recurring pound
of the heavy tide's kind explosions.

I wish I had her confidence.
In her black bathing suit
she even looks a little fat
and doesn't care,
perched on his lap while
he barely keeps from falling
off the sharp-edged rock.

I stand here on sand and try to hold
the camera still, catch their squinting
in the glare, their broad, bawdy smiles
that taunt me not to be so shy,
their little Jewish refugee.
They grin and I look at them
through the terrible shutter
which won't show I was here.

Sidewalk Art on Wall Street

You're not supposed to want the apple
in a Cezanne. Don't let your posters
from the museum match the divan.

But lenient Matisse! His art was meant
for the businessman—read store clerk or blue
collar, here—*as well as for the man*

of letters. This was long before the CEOs
existed, had spare homes decorated
with originals by a Matisse or a Van Gogh.

Not for the man who punched out his own Picasso—
Matisse said art should be *like an armchair*
and so, naturally, he'd have been down on Wall Street

painting the sidewalks with the college students.
He'd have garnered a few literate,
lovely-nippled girls to pose.

Their shirtless protests are aesthetic, too.
And of course the artist himself might have eaten
the apple which seems and is expensive.

Tortoise and Hare in the Museum

> Take the picture of my mother, exhibited at the Royal
> Academy as an "Arrangement in Grey and Black." Now that
> is what it is. To me it is interesting as a picture of my
> mother; but what can or ought the public do to care about
> the identity of the portrait?
> —James McNeill Whistler, *The Gentle Art of
> Making Enemies*

Once there was so much time it was like
a landscape painting that cleverly suggests
the vanishing of seeing with a tiny pencil point,
the top of an isosceles triangle wedged into the air
like a pyramid or an icicle. Discovered
in the Renaissance, perspective
can be played with, a Diebenkorn field
with a hint of the dashboard of a car
and one windshield wiper, or the car could be
someone's living room with a chair and picture window.
That mix of the abstract and the real
brings friends and lovers together like
good dance music or Rachmaninoff.
Art posters and used books on aesthetics
can make a party. For a while I'd actually arrived
at my dream from childhood and could do anything.
There's a time in life when you can almost hold still—
taste of a whittled slice of the richest cake.
I regarded the hours when I read Robbe-Grillet.
I was late to classes and ostentatiously stated
my age. Things will start to happen, regardless.
We find we're the object of someone's
observations, there's something terrible
we must be hiding, and we are the canvas stretched
onto wood, turning out to be good or not. Then try looking
at the time. I thought it was forever, that lying out
in the red clay by Lake Lanier, reading "The Idea of Order
at Key West." My stomach was flat then. I got sunburned.
I appreciated art, that's how I was, the woman at the well,

dawdling. I see, now, how some eyed me as if this were a race.
Names got made as fast as dandelions spring back.
I see how I needed to have an eye, always,
always on the clock, but I was reclining on Georgia clay,
vain as an odalisque, not seeing the point up there
in the painting, that timepiece in the sky like the moon,
like Jefferson's two-faced clock, one face hung outside
for those in the fields, the other keeping house
in the entryway with balanced cannonballs
that make the mechanism work like a minuet.
From where I was, the world was a salon—
then everyone was leaving. Whistler's mother
was a sport, sitting in for a model who was ill,
her son painting the musical light. Look close
and she is not what you thought. She is the figure
on whom light plays in *Arrangement in Grey and Black*.

The Painter at Noon

for Robert Tharsing and Ann Tower

Noon's upright light and a window's particular
angle invited back Renaissance perspective.
Resting by his great, leaning abstracts, he could see
across to the courthouse building and how people
return to a porch where they can smoke cigarettes—
in winter coats or skimpy blouses for humid minutes

before the air-conditioner's hum, life's minutes
used up in some office building, one's particular
task under fluorescent lighting. Their cigarettes,
the man's beret and slick pants and his perspective,
looking up at the skirts, one girl taking a pull
to light up, her two friends on either side—what he'd see

that made him paint them, he said, was how the scene
was always the same, right down to the minute,
the girl with the lighter always in the middle. These people
seemed composed in spite of their particular,
messy lives, their meetings stoic as the perspective
of faces on a bas-relief, except for the cigarettes.

But that was the juicy detail. Their need for cigarettes
arranged this constancy that made him see.
The blonde and the stacked girl called for 3-D perspective.
The painting is a souvenir of noon. Like Monet
obsessed with haystacks, he painted that particular
group—he was painting people

going through their lives. I saw where the people
used to stand and gossip, smoke their cigarettes.
I was at his studio window, and remember that particular
day, before reality set in. We were in a scene,
I felt, ourselves. I was alone with him for minutes,
I might have lost all perspective.

But who doesn't want the artist's perspective,
his view of her for a while? We were just people.
It was nothing, like someone taking a minute
off from work for a kiss or cigarette.
I was no match for his wife. Their place was a "scene."
They'd wear Hawaiian shirts at their fabulous parties.

Art was abstract, then, and people could flirt the minutes
away. His retrospective shows the sea, in particular,
but his brushwork could mean palmettos, cigarettes.

Available Beauty

The philosopher-kings are practicing
pirouettes on the art they deny—
they define "realism," for instance,
as assuming there is a field
to be described in the first place.
But meanwhile they can use,
as a cat-thief uses the roof he leaves behind,
the so-called field of poppies,
or maybe it was olive trees or sheaves
of wheat. The arguable field stands in
for what is not yet or what was last night,
like Van Gogh's whirling stars.

And so the painter must be sad—
that is the point of post-structuralism.
And the viewers, of course, must be sad too,
knowing they have missed the night at Arles forever.

I know that trying to trick the sublime
you hung your canvas like a coat
on a coat rack. And then where is there to go?
You and your wife go to Nova Scotia
and use the available beauty—
rocks copied with a monk's care for a manuscript,
a bleached whale's clavicle Ann found on the beach
and placed on a tablecloth next to a ruby-red vase.
She paints the stippled sea,
the spiny, violet lupins and the kindergarten sun,
brash and yellow on the Adirondack chairs.

Why did you paint these palm trees, I asked.
"Because they were there," you said, teasing me
about how I wanted certain things in a painting.
To be realistic, there is this crush I have

on you, so this must come out wrong, sound
like a crooning song, a boombox at the beach.
I bought your painting
which covers my living room wall,
big as the side of a room, an entrance
which the viewer cannot quite enter.

When both of us were married, and thirty,
you put your knee against my knee
in the restaurant in Kentucky.
But that was all that happened.
I can see the pond with water lilies
and the tall palm before the rented villa
in Italy, one of your sabbatical years.
I look, up close, at your representation
of a blue day in another country—
at the pink blossoms riding on the surface of the pond
and the palm tree's reflection inserted down into
the muddy interior. I think of the marsh king grabbing
the vain girl who doesn't want her shoes wet
and steps on a loaf of bread to get across.
But even this close there is nothing hidden—
the painting shows its work like open hands,
the magician demonstrating tricks to the kids.

Mars Black and Viridian play bass viol
against the lighter tones. The palm tree is doubled,
an echo shooting through the chartreuse and rosy pond.
Up in the hot, jeweled blue, clouds play
an octave of whites and Dove Grey hints
at improbable rain, hanging above
the towers and the clay roof tiles.
Little blobs of paint make flowers float,

the topiaries' lime-green edges
simple as two-by-fours, your painting showing
beauty is painting
and painting, beauty.

Time is always a trick. Your view of art
parallels how you take this bone cancer.
You do not flirt anymore
and shrug your shoulders when I ask
how you are, shrug and open your hands
and say, calmly, "It is out of my control,"
and open your hands.

IV

Her Art

I'd like to cry on Elizabeth Bishop's shoulder.
I lost my mother's engagement ring, for one thing.
Not your fault, she'd say. So much seems to want
to be lost. Even if, one day, in anger or grief
you threw it across the room or placed it somewhere
safe, the fact is, now, it's gone. Just read my poem.

Remember? My mother's watch was in that poem.
My losses are famous. Don't cry on anyone's shoulder—
even if I were available, I'm lost somewhere.
Find a nice shape and put your list of things
inside as you'd pack a valise. Be careful of your grief,
how you throw it around. People don't want

a sight like that. Write about your want
as if it were an apple or a moth. A poem,
if you're lucky, can help someone else's grief.
It might be there to lean on like a shoulder,
though that should not be your intent. My things—
why should you care at all for them or where

or why I lost them? You saw me, somewhere,
painting Florida, transcribing my want,
that perilous view, into some other thing.
It is not a raft for you to climb on. The poem
might be about someone else's shoulders,
how I miss them, perhaps, which is my grief,

not yours to worry over. Chart loss on a graph,
see how precisely rocks recall the wear
of tides and rain. Then think of those shoulders
you miss—pose them like a sculpture. The want
of arms made the Venus de Milo. A poem
is luck like that and discipline and things

you'll never have again. See those things
as tiles in a watercolor tin. Grief,
set right, can flicker and stay, and then the poem
can stand in for your lost ring. I cannot say where
to look for any of this, or if the friend you want
will disappear. Step into loss as you should—

as you like to step in water, somewhere, your shoulders
cold until you're swimming. My poem was a thing
I made, and it took some balancing, that grief and want.

Piano Legs

(Homage to Miss Mary Flannery O'Connor)

Her plots were engineered by God.
So naturally she wrote like hell,
free as shy Glenn Gould was, playing Bach,
a virtuoso we might dislike
were it not for the music.
To play so well you have to be
a little peculiar, cut
the romantics, those free
spirits, hum along with your recordings
proudly, mark your territory.

Just hear the notes in
the arpeggio, how they're spreading
out, more and more, until it's impossible,
like a peacock's embarrassing feathers,
a pianist's spread fingers across the octaves,
a hand on your leg. The body sways
upon the piano stool instead of dancing,
the artist absurdly sitting, pushing down keys
as a writer will press
the letters on a typewriter, trying
to express, express, express!

We hear Glenn Gould humming, moaning
in his love of Bach,
hear how the grandmother tries to connive
and wheedle her way into living.
She is unashamed of her false notes,
our heroine even if it doesn't sit right.

That story runs smoothly at first,
clipping along like a Bach
invention, like the miniature scene

in a well-made cuckoo clock. Wouldn't you like
to come be my little girl? asks the poor
waitress. Of course the rude girl snaps right back,
hard as a shot rubber band. The grandmother hisses.
She is not common, and enjoys, like a connoisseur,
the blue of Stone Mountain with its cut, Confederate
silhouettes. That little black boy outside the car window:
"Wouldn't that make a picture, now?"

But then the car falls right off the road
into a gully. Those kids we'd believe
are too mean to actually die get shot.
The Misfit comes back in the shirt
with parrots on it. Her son
just had that on. That yellow must hurt;
the birds must wheel in her eyes.
You could be one of my own children.

The cartoon has stopped and turned bloody.
But if you think about it this is what
they all wanted.
And look at the piano, curvy
and fat as an odalisque,
the huge body with its heartstrings
held up by just three legs,
like something beautiful and marred,
thick-ankled and mahogany.

And so we get the angry, educated girl
who knows she is ugly in others' eyes
and who doesn't love the Bible salesman,
but he still takes advantage of her.
The piano sits there so brazenly

with its bare, bowed legs
and Manley Pointer runs off with Hulga's
wooden leg instead of her virginity.

Who could call this grace? Miss O'Connor
has deftly left us at the scene
with just the Misfit to interview.
She is out in her yard in Georgia,
maneuvering her crutches,
feeding her peacocks who preen
and get their trains stuck underneath cars.
What's real is close to unbearable.

On Seeing a Photograph of Klimt's *Schubert at the Piano,* Destroyed by Fire

The tempo of the piece is there,
the glow and thrill, the lit gas lamps
and candles—the painting is on fire
as music is on fire sometimes.

Look at the girl with auburn hair, full
with the painter's child who dies, later,
her hair like tinsel in the light,
her dress made of roses.

The tenseness of the moment may be
why Klimt turned to the calmer thing.
His "decorative" later style disguises sex
as if it were not panting, sweating.

Flushed nudes hide beneath the pattern.
But listen to a Schubert composition,
all that beauty before he was thirty.
There he was, flaring, flaring—

thirteen symphonies without hearing one
played by an orchestra. Wanting the girl
whose parents won't approve of him. No money,
"The Trout Quintet" because he saw that fish,

rainbowing through the clear water, difficult
to catch, safe until the fisherman placed his boot
in, muddied the stream. Carousing with his friends
who called him "Little Mushroom"—

tamping down his genius like a cigarette.
So the plump man plays the pianoforte,
the painter hears his music and paints.
Everything rises in the picture's heat.

From Schubert's hands to the model's incandescent hair
you see the upward motion. The brush strokes writhe,
the painting has a brightness like the future.
It will be stolen, hidden at Schloss Immendorf.

The SS, retreating, had one night in those apartments,
drinking, sucking and fingering where
"Schubert at the Piano" and "Music" hung.
They left their fuses behind, and a timer.

Ode to Joy's Friend

> Joy's friend was an adolescent at the time of this observation. Such exuberant solicitations of petting by female dolphins, often with a strong sexual component, are most common at that age.
> —Rachel Smolker, *To Touch a Wild Dolphin*

The young dolphin who came around, sometimes, to play with Joy,
we named Joysfriend. She seemed like some kid next door, starved
for attention, and the two would race off to flirt with boys,
just like girls do on land. Joysfriend was from some other place,
not Monkey Mia, and only swam here to hang out with her friend,
who wasn't as wild as she. But that's the way adolescence

does you; you need a best friend when you're an adolescent—
it's required, like smiling in the hall, pretending joy
even when your heart is broken. So Joysfriend
and Joy would cruise "Shark's Bay" like those starved-
looking girls who wander through malls. They'd find places
to pick up seaweed and sponges and get near boys.

Joysfriend didn't mind if she seemed, to those lazy boys,
a little too easy. She was happy and didn't know about adult sins
or getting a reputation. She imagined the sea as a place
beyond such quandaries. She must have had a word for joy
that is sky-blue and sweeter than ours, which to us and our starved
senses would only sound like a squeal. And so she liked friends,

and the guys tolerated her, fingered her, told their friends.
Joy may have warned her about those boys—
they only loved Holeyfin, Joy's mother—they were still starved
for her. After all these years it was she who roused their senses,
she who brought them the sea's salty joy—
even with that old bullet hole, that ruined place

on her fin. Even dolphins will exclude those from another place—
they have their faults, like any other incomprehensible friend.
They like what they are used to. They get their joy

from local things, familiar women—a "young boy's
club" of the sea. Anyway, they don't need adolescent,
needy girls—they're not that sex-starved.

Joysfriend, though, could hardly have felt starved
when she lay on that sea, showed off her belly, rubbed places
that felt good against the male dolphins' fins. That "adolescent"
we'd observed as "exuberant." We cheered her on like friends
as she swam past us, a silver mirror flashing between bell buoys.
We'd felt that ache. We knew about Beethoven's "Ode to Joy"—

his syphilis, his starved ears, the fierce applause of friends.
He didn't hear the stopped choir of adolescent boys.
Music was some farther place—*dal segno al fine*—in his notes on joy.

House Cats

Our bed is their savannah, where
she leans against his belly, snuggles in.
Neutered before he got the chance
to know, he knows anyway
and bites her neck, plays rough enough
she must jump off the bed. He follows,
wild with something not quite hunger,
being rubbed, licking someone's ice cream bowl.
It's somewhere behind, in time and space,
a buzz between his shoulder blades,
some delicacy he can't quite scope
as he has the distance from the refrigerator
to the top of the highest kitchen cabinet,
warm with track lights, inches from
the solid white top of this square world.

He gets what he wants, usually,
swings on a doorknob until the door
moves, lets him in—otherwise he can knock
small things off their bedside table—
fingernail polish, sertraline, sleeping
pills, a curvy glass he dips his paw into
for water. A gymnast, a physicist,
a thirsty anthropologist, he dips into
what was once plain river. He turns
the drinking glass into what it was.
He knows he is adored,
though he does not care why.
"Leonine," they say. His pride
is made up of those who roar
when he leaps around corners on the banister
the way he'd stroll through the branches of trees.
The anxious ones stare when he sucks and pulls
his needle of a penis with its tiny thorns, set to trap,

to titillate. An ancient rumble is lodged
in his throat. Too much heavy
petting—when she licks and cleans
his ears—makes him almost smell some life
that is primordial, useless. The jungle on the quilt
stays sewn into place.

"Rosebud," He Whispered

Rosebud, of course, was her clitoris.
See how sexual it looks on the sled,
pursed but also reaching,
more like a tulip, really, a little hand
grasping, wanting to clutch,
its drooping, languorous, coy design
that waits to be plucked and sucked.

So how could the great director resist
such a trite and famous
endearment, its multifold and useful
associations and democratic
thrust, the innocent little rose imprint
an American kid could sit on to ride down
a slope of snow, the red sled sliding,
slipping, the way when your hands are cold
you can't hold on to a thing, the way
life always goes, the tragic arc?
And so Orson Welles could not help hearing
of that fetching image
and knowing how his film would be set off,
such momentum and velocity carrying
the narrative and also the director's career
careening downward, everything more
than the sum of its parts, turned on that flexible,
athletic metaphor, *le mot juste*
that would blossom and snowball
all the way down from the man's directing
of *Citizen Kane* to his acting
in a commercial for Paul Masson rosé wine.
I used to take my wine glass and click it against
the glass screen of the television. That slight
image, white on a red sled, little red tongue
in the icy cold—such honest transport is hard to steer
as it takes you, headlong, where it will.

Stanislavsky's Method

She plays the kind of woman she would chide
and disapprove of on her show. And so
I see the person she would be if she'd let go.
I see her flirting, unafraid, not shuttered.

The light is on the angles of her face.
She lights a cigarette like she's a pro
and stands there, curvy in her yellow dress.
When Oprah acts she lets herself go,

sure of the script as a rein in case
she sings too well as the butler's wife.
She hits so close to why a person fails
I think of Rembrandt, his palette knife's

rowdy excursions, riding a jaw's curve
down into the shadows, unreconciled
places. You let yourself almost fall
backward, but that's Stanislavsky's method.

Handling Her Clothes

Even Henry James could be stupid.
However perfect his pitch, hearing
how a word slows the air like a shutter
and meanings get bandied about
like a shuttlecock in the humid air,

the change of key, the fan
of tones like a coloratura's in an opera,
notes like the purples in a peacock's feathers,
the shifting hand of cards,
in the air the stunning
misunderstandings, curves and sides
of words that will flail
and fishtail;

however he could limn where a thing
goes wrong, the jaw line blurring
as precisely as in Sargent's watercolors,
his portraits built of water and light,
the strap of a woman's gown falling—

it was different with this friend, close-up,
unwieldy and awful. He wrote his brother
about that nearly "fatal" day. Years later
a story with which he'd regale company—
her skirts like "vast, black balloons."

They had been close, traveled together,
Alice writing, "he's off again flirting
with Fenimore." He'd confided in her,
reclined in their talk like it was a nice chaise-longue.

Then she chose to dive from her rooms in Venice,
straight onto the paving stones. It looked like
someone's white clothing until a servant heard
her moaning. She had just asked for a glass
of milk, had written a note asking her old friend
to throw her wardrobe into the lagoon.
He'd have to touch what he'd despise
touching. Her request was so brave
and careless, of course she had figured
out this scene, beforehand:

Henry and his gondolier, handling
her clothes. They had rowed
a long way out for this private matter.
How he must have blushed,
there in a scene of his colleague's devising—
a writer, herself, an inventor of the good plots
they once laughed about like conspirators
when she—not he—
had been the famous "author."

She used to walk the marshes in Florida
and must have known the qualities
of this heavy, luscious water,
how serenely and reluctantly it would consider
such gifts, and then how the coy green
would push back with its mermaid fingers,
repelled by the fuss of men
beginning to sweat and appear desperate,
their stooping and prodding with poles and oars
at the stuff that kept rising,
such optimistic, billowing materials,
organdy, silk, poplin.

It is pleasant, from a distance,
to imagine those awful water lilies, floating away
from the Venetian lions, making a scene.
Her low-cut gowns, their resurrections,
by the time they all did finally sink they'd bobbed up
far too many times—those wired shapes,
corsets and lace, in which she'd stayed her soul—
her anger, her bodices, her little shoes, her camisoles.

How a Poem Can Staunch a Wound

Writing it, finding some music or metaphor
which, on its own, takes surprisingly off—
the concept distracting like a balsa-wood frame
that can lift from the earth for a while, glide through
insect territory, blue-green wings netted like tutus,
the tremulous fireflies' lemony bulbs, wavering,
near-sighted in the arbitrary, tall, dangerous air
which also carries a radio-control tower's terrifying
signals, the sand in the eye, the body preoccupied
by flight, the dark speed outside an oval window,
the passengers' comfort, pillows for their necks
and the necessary, whistling air pressure—
I can feel, sometimes, elated.

But for a time the old master, Walt Whitman,
did the impossible, walked on the ground,
muddy, in Washington, let go, completely,
his tissue-paper poems. His mind got soaked
with the bright blood on the grass everywhere,
too many for the hospital so they set up tents,
a young soldier's face turned away not to look
at the stump, the free-spirited poet with his sleeves
rolled up to swab out the "offensive" matter.
Those young men who'd fallen as oddly as Icarus—
they sometimes kissed his bearded lips
and called him, gratefully, "Mother."

A Piece of Work

> *She had*
> *A heart—how shall I say?—too soon made glad,*
> *Too easily impressed; she liked whate'er*
> *She looked on, and her looks went everywhere.*
>   —Robert Browning, "My Last Duchess"

Here's the cock-tease, in this photo.
We took these pictures of the job site,
before and after, to show how good
our work is, but I snuck in a shot of her
when she wasn't looking. Get a load
of that—see the low-cut blouse?
That material was thin.
You can almost see her nipples poking through.

I swear it was that or better every day.
The whole job took two years, off and on.
The picture is her in her kitchen
before we put in the cabinets.
She wanted them all glassed-in,
and I told her she wouldn't want that
everywhere. You need a place for cereal,
hamburger helper, what not.
She kept insisting, but I knew
her ideas weren't practical.

She's the type that don't wear a bra—
liberal, one of them feminists, I guess.
Well, she wouldn't get up till noon.
A couple times I knocked on her bedroom
door just to make sure she was alive.
I'd ask, *didn't she have her class to go to?*
She'd thank me, say no, she taught Tuesdays,
Thursdays—or was it the other way around?
I'd hope for a peek back then,
but she'd be holding the sheet up to her neck.

She'd lost her husband—a professor.
That gives people airs, usually,
but she didn't act too good for me.
She kept on offering things—coffee,
Coke when it was hot. Even an antique icebox
that had one broken leg. "I'll never
get around to fixing it," she said.
I have it in my living room, now. Here, come look.
See that lovely oak, that grain? Run your hands
over that. It didn't take two hours
to get that little leg back on straight.

She felt "overwhelmed," she told me,
and talked like we were friends.
Once she cried in front of me and my men.
When a woman acts that loose and sweet
what does she expect? She got so she would hug me
goodbye. She smiled at everyone.

I'd lock her and her kids in when I left
the house. You get so you feel protective,
and I knew she had some woman stalking
her house. Oh yeah—she even told me she'd had
an affair. We'd talk like that. I told her I liked
make-up sex and she laughed.
We traded our favorite Italian restaurants.
Hers was "Scotti's," that old place downtown.
She liked how they had wine bottles with candle wax
hanging from the ceiling. No, I said, the best place
is this little dive I know, on the west side.
But I'm a real Italian. I know what's good
without it being in the restaurant guide.

They'd had that order for storm doors
in for a while. I hadn't seen her in months.
She'd married that guy she had the affair
with. So now she can put on airs?

I could tell she was ready to hug me
when I came to the door. "So how is your wife?"
Well, the wife left me last year,
although I didn't tell her that. I shrugged,
figured she'd get the message.
She told me she'd just made coffee.
I said I thought I smelled something good,
but didn't know where the cups were kept
these days. She followed me in. It was when
I asked her how she liked the marble-topped island.
I'd cut that marble for her right out in the yard.
She put her hand on it and said
she loved it. I said, "I missed you—you miss me?"

She started in with one of her prissy little hugs.
I hugged her back but tighter, started kissing
her cheek, then her mouth.
I forced my tongue in and felt her breasts,
her nice big ass.

She was so still and passive—
like a rabbit when you catch hold.
Started talking real fast and polite—
what a bad idea when we were such friends,
this would *kill* her husband! I said, "We don't hafta
tell him." I was hard, too, and letting
her know it through our clothes.
What a stuck-up bitch. My consolation prize
was pulling out her leotard top,
fingering those nipples.
And then I let her go.

I went and poured my coffee. "You all right?"
I asked. And she said sure.
Then she went upstairs somewhere
and must have called her husband.
He came home fast, didn't even frown,
the coward. They left in a hurry
and I didn't finish the door
any better than I had to.

The boss told me what she said I did
and I said, "You know how looney
that woman is."
I'd never have thought she'd be so low.
That's my *job* she was talking about.
Hey, want a cold beer, Neighbor?

The Woman Who Was Almost My Sister-in-Law

(After Hemingway's "Montparnasse")

There are never any suicides in the quarter among people one knows
No successful suicides.

There are no broken jaws and bruises on the arms
of those one knows at work or meets at Starbucks for coffee.
There is news online, though, about the woman
a Louisiana sheriff blamed
for not having a concealed gun license
when her estranged husband beat her to death with a baseball bat.
That's tricky, though, considering that woman in Florida
who got sentenced to twenty years for "standing her ground."
Her husband had knocked the bathroom door down,
locked the garage doors, even, so she could not get away.
Her children said it was just a warning shot. But there you are.
They said it was because her children were in the house.
The rules you have to follow are as crazy as a maze.

There are examples we can see on "Dr. Phil."
A beautiful blonde—I mean you can tell that she *was*
beautiful—went on the show to let people know this violence
is real. She was wearing an artificial eye.

"If you have this baby, I'll never leave you alone"
is what my first husband said.
So I had an abortion
and then I got away from him.
A friend of mine had said, "I wonder what your life will be
ten years from now." That also helped me get away.

Years later I was looking on Google
for people I used to know. I finally typed his name.
I found it in a news story about his younger brother,
who'd been murdered by his wife.
She would have been my sister-in-law if I had stayed married.

She was an English major like I had been,
and he and that brother had the same ice-blue eyes.
They were both beautiful men, and she must have felt
like I did when I was nineteen. Her neighbors
were shocked. They'd known there had been some trouble—
the police had been called and he'd been in jail a few times.
She'd had a black eye the last time they saw her
and she'd had some excuse like being clumsy.
She used to leave brownies on the porch for their kids.

I never met this clumsy woman
who seems to have embodied the end of my story—
if I hadn't escaped from that story.

It is difficult to picture the killing itself.
The police said his entrails were on the kitchen floor.
I don't think I could have killed my first husband like that.
I think I would have been the one murdered, unless—
there were things the court kept secret from the public.
They had a daughter—eighteen—and what they did report
was that she talked about how he treated
their beagle puppies. And she said
she'd asked her friends if they knew someone with a gun—
she wanted to put "a contract" out on her father.
She was out with friends the night it happened.

Her mother said that something "just snapped." There was
a sledge hammer out in the yard and she'd brought it in
for some reason, she didn't know why. And he was asleep.
She hit him with the sledge hammer. But then he woke up,
and she got the kitchen knife because now she was done for.
Her own wounds, the police said, seem to have been self-inflicted.

I was embarrassed, in those days, out in public
with two black eyes and a swollen jaw. People frowned at me
as if I were an accomplice to my own injury.
Really, there is very little one can do in certain situations.
But whatever was not divulged in the case
must be why the woman, who would have been my sister-in-law,
got a shortened sentence.

"Every afternoon," writes Hemingway,
"the people one knows can be found at the café."
There are people I could meet for coffee at Starbucks
who really wouldn't care to hear my story.

The Danger of These Lines You Wrote

>   Therefore,
>   Their sons grow suicidally beautiful
>   At the beginning of October,
>   And gallop terribly against each other's bodies

is how they make football like Autumn,
roaring down to its tragic goal line
in a knuckle-splitting, skidding glissando,

or like my sister playing Prokofiev at thirteen
in a short skirt up on stage when I heard
the comment, "she plays like she isn't a virgin."

I think you hit some primal key that makes us feel
we're in a dance, a turning in air above the ferns,
like Prokofiev's concerto hitting close to fossil nerve.

When she played with the Chautauqua Symphony,
my sister got blood on the piano keys,
those lines written to sound like three hands

in the cadenza. Arpeggios, hand crossings,
my prodigy sister. We listened,
in the practice cabin, her boyfriend placing the needle

on the record, for the orgasm near the end
of the Rachmaninoff Second. But which place?
Was that it? The music got better and better—

how could we know where it ended?
That is what I'm saying about your poem.
Your dad slaving at the glass factory,

my mother throwing her ruby red glassware,
"moondrops," in the garbage. It reminded her, she said,
of being poor. "Hazel-Atlas Glass" gleams in your poems,

a folk melody begins the wild concerto.
And so a line of music or a line in your poem
is misleading. To be so vulnerable and romantic—

Prokofiev had stage fright when he played that part.
Your word, "Therefore," is a bright container
turned lavender in the sun. Regardless,

just upriver in Steubenville, football players,
caught on video, laugh as they fumble and finger-fuck
the dreams of a passed-out teenaged girl.

                (after James Wright's "Autumn Begins in Martin's Ferry, Ohio")

A Note from the Author

"Hattiesburg," "June 1969," and "Rescuing My Sister" began as exercises I wrote and posted in response to prompts from David Lehman and Angela Ball on *The American Scholar Online*. My thanks to them and to my fellow contributors.

I want to thank the following writers, teachers, editors, and friends, all of whom contributed to this journey of a book: Philip Appleman, Don Bogen, Mary Burgan, Stephen Corey, James Cummins, Marilyn Hacker, Judith Hall, Andrew Hudgins, Roger Mitchell, James Naremore, Edgar Slotkin, Maura Stanton, and William Trowbridge. Thanks to the friends who read my manuscript early on—Barbara Elovic, Maureen Bloomfield, Aliki Barnstone, Liz Rosenberg, T.R. Hummer, Mark Andres (who let me use one of his fine paintings for the cover)—and to the beautiful art colony of Facebook friends I am lucky to be a part of. I am so appreciative of the generosity of Pamela Johnson Parker, Simon Evnine, Kathryn Kopple, Sophia Kartsonis, and Lesley Jenike, each of whom published or wrote kindly about my work on a website, blog or online magazine. I am grateful to Kevin Morgan Watson, the publisher of Press 53, for his beautiful design of my book.

Thanks, of course, to my in-house editor and wonderful poet and husband, John Philip Drury. Thanks to my sister, Susan Walters, and to my brother-in-law, Jeff Moore, for their intelligent and generous comments, through the years, on my writing.

This book has finally happened because of Pam Uschuk's and William Pitt Root's generous reading of the manuscript and their acceptance of it as a part of the Silver Concho Poetry Series. Thank you so much, my beautiful benefactors!

LaWanda Walters grew up in Mississippi and North Carolina. She earned her B.A. at the University of North Carolina in Chapel Hill, an M.A. in Literature from California State University at Humboldt, and an M.F.A. in Poetry from Indiana University, where she won the Academy of American Poets Prize. Her poems have appeared in *The Antioch Review*, *The Cincinnati Review*, *Cutthroat*, *The Georgia Review*, *The Laurel Review*, *North American Review*, *Ploughshares*, *Shenandoah*, *Southern Poetry Review*, and *Sou'wester*. Her poem "Marilyn Monroe" appears in *Obsession: Sestinas in the Twenty-First Century* (Dartmouth College Press, 2014). "Goodness in Mississippi" was chosen by Sherman Alexie for *Best American Poetry 2015*. She is the mother of two grown children, Tess Despres Weinberg and Sean Jason Weinberg, and lives with her husband, John Drury, in Cincinnati.

About the Cover Artist

Mark Andres is a painter and filmmaker who lives in Portland, Oregon.

www.ingramcontent.com/pod-product-compliance
Lightning Source LLC
LaVergne TN
LVHW041339080426
835512LV00006B/533